A New True Book

SPACE SHUTTLES

Friskey

TABLE OF CONTENTS

CHILDRENS PRESS, CHICAGO

THE COLUMBIA

The countdown clock
ticks away the final
seconds. T-minus
5-4-3-2-1 . . .
The rocket engines roar.
The space shuttle,
Columbia, lifts off.

The *Columbia* is a new idea in space travel. It is a space shuttle. Unlike earlier spacecraft, the *Columbia* can go into space and come back again and again.

Because a space shuttle
can go back and forth,
many things will be
possible.

People and materials
can be carried into space.
And returned.

It will be possible to
build a settlement in space
someday.

Someday people will build and live in space colonies like the one shown below. They will travel into space and return to Earth on regular space shuttle flights.

THE SPACE SHUTTLE

The space shuttle travels at great speeds. It can go from the United States to Europe in less than 20 minutes. In eight minutes it can cross the continent of North America.

The space shuttle lands like a glider. Its engines are not used.

The shuttle takes off like
a rocket. But it lands like
a glider.

Its three rocket engines
are used only in the lift-off.
The shuttle needs the
great force of the rockets
to boost it beyond the pull
of the Earth's gravity.

The space shuttle stands on its launching pad. You can see its big fuel tank and rocket boosters.

Fuel for the three main engines is carried piggy-back in an enormous tank.

Two rocket boosters are fastened to the sides of the fuel tank. They add to the thrust of the three main engines.

The two rocket boosters cut away from the shuttle in space. At this point in the flight the shuttle is traveling about 3,213 miles per hour.

These rockets burn for two minutes. Then they are cut loose. They drop by parachutes into the ocean. They are picked up by ship and used again.

The big empty fuel tank
is dropped later. It breaks
up in space. It is not used
again.

Now two smaller rear
engines take over. They
boost the shuttle into orbit
around the Earth.

There are more than
thirty small thrusters all
around the shuttle. These
are used for speed
changes, balance, and
direction control.

View of the shuttle's two-level cabin. The flight deck is on the upper level. The crew's living quarters are below.

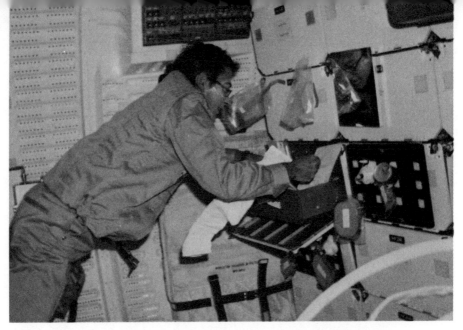

Astronaut John Young, the commander of the *Columbia's* first flight, finishes shaving in zero gravity. A food tray is mounted on the locker door at right to keep it from floating in space.

INSIDE THE SPACE SHUTTLE

The shuttle is built to carry seven people. They live in a climate just like Earth's in a two-level cabin.

Commander and pilot of the space shuttle will always be astronauts. The others probably will be experts in the work to be done.

The flight deck is on the upper level. Either the commander or pilot can use the controls. Or computers on Earth can take over the job of guiding the space shuttle.

The living quarters are below the flight deck.

The space shuttle is not a simple machine. It is an electronic wonder.

A workman checks some of the space shuttle's electronic equipment.

Flight deck controls

There are more than 200 "black boxes" throughout the shuttle. There are more than 2,000 switches, too.

There are many controls in the flight deck. Some are used for the work done in the cargo bay.

With its cargo bay open the shuttle can put satellites into Earth orbit.

The cargo bay of the shuttle is about as big as a railroad boxcar. Its doors open up like the shells of a clam.

Picture of the cargo bay taken from the *Columbia's* flight deck during its first space mission.

Workers in space suits can enter the cargo bay through an air-lock tunnel. In the cargo bay they work in almost weightless ease. Remember the shuttle is flying outside the pull of Earth's gravity. Things that are very heavy on Earth weigh very little in space.

The mechanical arm of the space shuttle is used to move
objects in and out of its cargo bay.

Skylab II took this photograph of Skylab I (above) in Earth orbit.
Skylab III later photographed this hurricane (below) forming over
the Atlantic Ocean.

WORKING IN SPACE

Already there are hundreds of unmanned satellites circling the Earth. They affect our lives every day.

A weather satellite helps tell what our weather will be. It can track a hurricane and save many lives.

Scientists prepare the world's first commercial maritime telecommunications satellite that was sent into space in 1976.

There are communication satellites, too. People in North America can watch a soccer game in Italy as though they had ringside seats. People in Germany or Japan can watch the World Series as the games are played.

One satellite can give a ship its exact position in thirty seconds in any kind of weather.

Another photographs the Earth. It can cover hundreds of square miles in seconds.

Infrared photograph of the mouth of the Colorado River in northern Baja, California and Sonora, Mexico as seen from a spacecraft in Earth orbit.

The shuttle's arm reaches up to pull a satellite into its cargo bay.

The space shuttle crews will be able to fix these satellites in space.

The great arm of the cargo carrier can reach out and bring one of them aboard.

The spacelab (above) was built to fit into the shuttle's cargo bay.
Below: Someday working space stations, based on scientific concepts
tested by the spacelab, will be built.

Scientists can work on it in the cargo bay. If necessary, the satellite can be taken to Earth to be fixed. Then it can be returned to space.

With the shuttle, workers can build solar power stations in space. At these stations sunlight could be changed to electricity and beamed to Earth for use.

THE SPACELAB

One of the most important payloads carried by the shuttle will be its spacelab. This has been built by ten European countries.

The spacelab fits into the shuttle's cargo bay. It has its own crew section. Here scientists can work without space suits. They

Inside the space shuttle and spacelab, workers do not have to wear space suits.

can go through an air-lock
tunnel into the forward
cabin under the flight
deck.

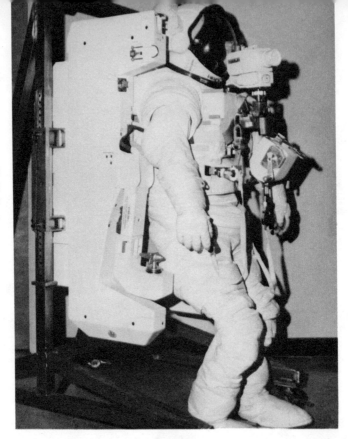

To work outside the shuttle, workers must wear space suits.

To work in the open section of the lab, they will have to wear space suits.

Spacelab scientists will conduct experiments in medicine and manufacturing.

Lifelines keep the astronauts hooked to the shuttle. Without these lifelines the astronauts would drift into space.

The shuttle can be flown directing its instruments toward the Earth. They will scan the Earth for its minerals, pollution, water resources, crop diseases, and many other things.

Scientist-astronaut Anna L. Fisher trains for future space shuttle missions.

Astronaut-pilot Robert L. Crippen, on the first space shuttle mission,
did some acrobatics in zero gravity while *Columbia* was in Earth orbit.

SPACELAB WORKERS

Spacelab work is open to men and women of all nations. They need not be astronauts. But they must have some special training. There are zero gravity exercises. There is training in space-flight housekeeping.

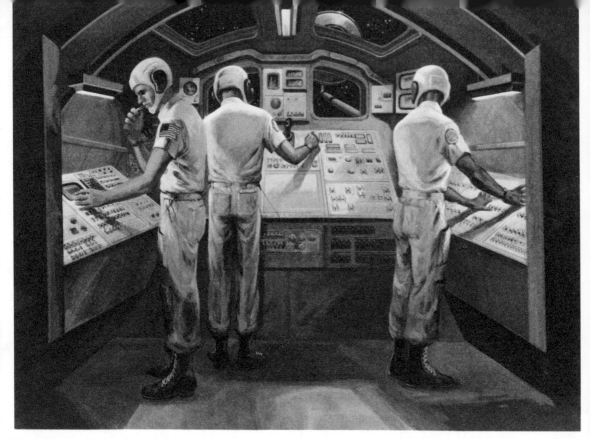

The shuttle has six windows wrapped around the front and sides for full vision. There are two overhead windows and two windows behind the flight deck overlooking the cargo bay.

In space they will work in the lab from 7 to 30 days. When off duty, they live in the crew cabin.

Special heat-resistant tiles were developed and used in the *Columbia.*

SPACE PRODUCTS

Many things in our daily lives already have come from the space program. Pocket calculators, microwave ovens, and digital watches came from the space program.

Today the heat-resistant materials used in the fireman's clothes (above) and the advanced equipment used to take a sonar picture of a baby's heart (below) were first developed for the space program.

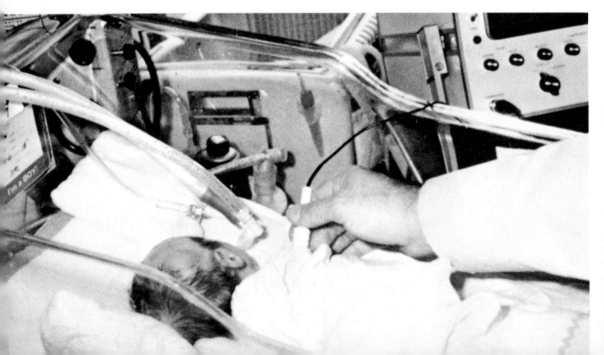

Lighter, warmer clothes and better fire-fighting equipment have been made, too.

The pacemakers and all kinds of health-care tools also have been developed.

And that is not the half of it. With the space shuttle and its spacelab more and more things will be discovered.

You may never choose
to settle in a space colony.
But you may someday take
a trip that is out of this
world. You may be a
passenger or worker on
the amazing space shuttle
that goes back and forth
in and out of space.

WORDS YOU SHOULD KNOW

air-lock —a place where the same amount of air is kept under pressure

astronaut —a person trained to fly in a spacecraft

beamed (BEEMD) —sent out

black box —a place where the parts that make something work are located

boost   to lift by pushing

cargo bay —a place where things are stored

climate (CLY • mit) —temperature, weather conditions

colony —a place where a group of people would live together

commander (kuh • MAN • der) —person in charge; leader

computer (kum • PYOO • ter) —a machine that works with high-speed electronics to solve problems

electronic (ee • lek • TRON • ik) —run by electricity

enormous (ee • NOR • mus) —very, very big; huge

fuel (FYOOL) —anything that is burned to give off heat or energy

gravity (GRAV • ih • tee) —the force that the earth and other heavenly bodies have that pulls other things toward their center

living quarters (LIV • ing KWAR • terz) —the rooms in which people live

manufacture (man • yoo • FAC • chur) —to make a product

orbit (OR • bit) —the path that something takes in space

payload (PAY • lode) —cargo that can be used for a very good purpose

rear —back part of something

satellite (SAT • el • lite) —a body that orbits in space

settle —to make a home or place to live in

thrust —to push hard

thruster —small engines to push a spacecraft

zero gravity —a place where there is no force of gravity